KU-037-865

Journeys

Paul Mason

Heinemann
LIBRARY

www.heinemann.co.uk/library

Visit our website to find out more information about **Heinemann Library** books.

To order:

☎ Phone 44 (0) 1865 888066

▤ Send a fax to 44 (0) 1865 314091

▭ Visit the Heinemann Bookshop at www.heinemann.co.uk/library to browse our catalogue and order online.

First published in Great Britain by Heinemann Library, Halley Court, Jordan Hill, Oxford OX2 8EJ, part of Harcourt Education. Heinemann is a registered trademark of Harcourt Education Ltd.

Editorial: Jilly Attwood and Claire Throp
Design: David Poole and Geoff Ward
Picture Research: Rosie Garai and Su Alexander
Production: Séverine Ribierre

Originated by Ambassador Litho Ltd
Printed in Hong Kong by Wing King Tong

ISBN 0 431 17713 9
07 06 05 04 03
10 9 8 7 6 5 4 3 2 1

British Library Cataloguing in Publication Data

Mason, Paul
Journeys - (Rites of Passage)
394
A full catalogue record for this book is available from the British Library.

Acknowledgements

The publishers would like to thank the following for permission to reproduce photographs: Corbis pp. **4** (Gavriel Jecan), **5** (David Samuel Robbins), **6** (Carmen Redondo), **7**, **12** (Hanan Isachar), **9** (Nik Wheeler), **11** (Jacques M. Chenet), **13** (James Marshall), **16** (Albrecht G. Schaefer), **17** (Roman Soumar), **23**, **27** (Galen Rowell), **25** (L. Clarke), **26** (Michael St. Maur Sheil), **28** (Derek Croucher); Corbis/Eye Ubiquitous pp. **10** (Chris Bland), **18** (Bennett Dean); Getty Images p. **20** (Nabeel Turner); Magnum p. **29** (Steve McCurry); Magnum/Abbas p. **21**; Mary Evans p. **14**; Panos p. **19** (Daniel O'Leary); Robert Harding p. **15** (Photri Inc); Tibet Images p. **22** (Jirina Simajchlova); Travel Ink p. **24** (Abbie Enock)

Cover photograph of worshippers circling the Kaaba in Saudi Arabia, reproduced with permission of Getty Images/Nabeel Turner.

The publishers would like to thank both the Interfaith Education Centre, Bradford and Georga Godwin for their assistance in the preparation of this book.

Disclaimer

All the Internet addresses (URLs) given in this book were valid at the time of going to press. However, due to the dynamic nature of the Internet, some addresses may have changed, or sites may have ceased to exist since publication. While the author and publishers regret any inconvenience this may cause readers, no responsibility for any such changes can be accepted by either the author or the publishers.

Every effort has been made to contact copyright holders of any material reproduced in this book. Any omissions will be rectified in subsequent printings if notice is given to the publishers.

Contents

Any words printed in bold letters, **like these**,
are explained in the Glossary.

Special journeys

There are lots of different kinds of journey. Most journeys are very ordinary. When you go to the supermarket in the car, for example, there is probably nothing special about the trip. But some journeys *are* special. This book is about these special journeys and the reasons why people make them.

Religious journeys

Some journeys are special because they are an important part of a religion. These are called **pilgrimages**. Some people go on a pilgrimage because it is their religious duty. **Muslims**, for example, are supposed to visit their most **holy** city, Makkah, at least once in their life if possible.

On many pilgrimages the journey itself is as important as the place where it ends. Tibetan **Buddhists** in China follow special routes on their pilgrimages to various holy sites, for example. So do **Christian** pilgrims visiting Santiago de Compostela in Spain.

Pilgrims bathe in the River Ganges. Many have journeyed hundreds of miles to get there.

Other journeys

Some special journeys are not linked to religion at all. For example, in 1911 the explorer R. F. Scott set off with a team of men to try to reach the South Pole. They hoped to be the first people to get there. Scott's attempt to be first to the Pole failed and he and his men died, but they became a **symbol** of the spirit of bravery and exploration.

These flags in the Himalayan mountains have prayers written on them. People believe the wind carries the prayers to Heaven.

Rites of passage

In 1909, a man called Arnold van Gennep wrote about rites of passage, which mark important moments of change in a person's life. He said there are three changes in every rite of passage:

- leaving one group
- moving on to a new stage
- and joining a new group.

Bible journeys

The Bible tells of many journeys. Among the most important are those made leading up to the birth of Jesus in Bethlehem.

This close-up shows part of the site of the Nativity in Bethlehem, Israel, where Jesus is believed to have been born.

Mary and Joseph

One of the first journey-stories tells of the arrival of Mary and Joseph, Jesus's mother and father. They had to travel to Bethlehem to register themselves in a census (population count). When they arrived it was impossible to find an inn for the night. Mary and Joseph ended up sleeping in a stable with the animals. This is where Jesus was born.

Today, many **Christians** visit Bethlehem, especially at Christmas. They go there to remember the birth of Jesus. One of the most popular places to visit is the Church of the Nativity. This stands in the spot were Jesus is thought to have been born. A **Mass** is said outside at midnight, and the area is always full of people.

The wise men and the shepherds

Another story tells of a group of shepherds who arrived soon after Jesus' birth, having been told to come by an angel. They had travelled down from their flocks of sheep in the hills to welcome the Son of God to Earth. Men from far away also came to bring gifts for the newborn baby, Jesus.

Today many Christian travellers visit the Shepherds' Fields, where the angel is said to have appeared. People visit all year, but the site is especially popular at Christmas.

This is a procession of Greek Orthodox Christians at Christmas time in Bethlehem.

Sarah's story

Sarah, now eleven years old, remembers her visit to Shepherds' Fields:

'I went to Shepherds' Fields with my family when I was five. It was Christmas time, and I remember feeling amazed. I was standing there in the very spot where an angel appeared to the shepherds. There were loads of other people there too, but it was still easy to imagine.'

The Way of St James

One of the oldest pilgrim routes in Europe is the *Camino de Santiago*. This is Spanish for the 'Way of St James'. The ancient path ends at the Spanish city of Santiago de Compostela. This is where the remains of St James, one of the twelve **apostles**, are said to lie.

The journey to Santiago first became popular more than 1000 years ago. The Bishop of Le Puy, in France, was one of the first to make the trip in 950 CE. People went to Santiago to see and touch the bones of the saint. They believed that the saint would help them speak to God and ask forgiveness for their **sins**. Today, the journey has become a celebration for many **Christians**.

The Camino de Santiago is said to start at Saint-Jean-Pied-de-Port and end at Santiago. But a network of routes from across Europe feeds pilgrims towards the start of the path.

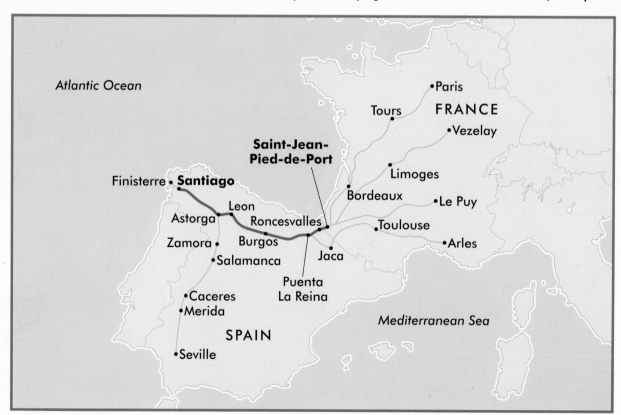

These pilgrims on the Way of St James are kneeling with crosses at the pass of Roncesvalles in Spain.

The Way of St James goes 800 kilometres from the foothills of the Pyrenean mountains to Santiago. Most people begin their journey at Roncesvalles. There are special places for pilgrims to rest along the way. It takes most people a month to complete the journey.

Evelyn's story

Evelyn Lapasset walked part of the Way of St James when she was fourteen years old:

'I walked the route in two parts, the second part one year after the first. We began in Saint-Jean-Pied-de-Port the first year and finished in Burgos. It was very hard, but fun to meet all the other people on the journey.'

Christian journeys

Hundreds of thousands of **Christians** visit the Holy Land every year. This is an area of land that is now mainly in Israel, at the eastern edge of the Mediterranean Sea. **Jews** and **Muslims** also visit the Holy Land, as many of their **holy** sites are in this area too.

One of the most popular places for Christians to visit is the city of Jerusalem, where Jesus preached many of his lessons. Important sites within Jerusalem include the Mount of Olives and the Garden of Gethsemane. Many Christians visit the Praetorium, the building where Jesus was tried and found guilty. They may also follow Jesus' journey through the streets carrying the cross to the place where he was **crucified**.

Lourdes

Each year about 3 million Christians travel to Lourdes, France. They go there mainly because they hope to be cured of sicknesses. Christian pilgrims have visited the town since 1858, when a fourteen-year-old girl named Bernadette Soubirous had a series of visions of the **Virgin Mary** in a grotto (small cave) nearby. The young girl was later made a saint.

This chapel at Lourdes was built because of the miracles that Christians believe happened there. Today many people journey to the chapel hoping to be cured of sickness.

Pope John Paul II, who became Pope in 1978, is a great traveller himself. He visits many countries so that Catholics around the world, who can not afford to visit Rome, can see him.

Rome

Another popular place of **pilgrimage** for Christians is Rome, Italy. The Roman Catholic branch of Christianity has its headquarters there, in The Vatican City. The head of the Catholic Church is the Pope, who is thought to be God's representative on Earth. People gather in Rome to hear the Pope say **Mass** from a balcony of the Vatican.

Walsingham pilgrimage

There is a legend that in 1061, in Walsingham, England, a woman named Richeldis de Faverches had a vision. In it, she journeyed to the house in the Holy Land where the Angel Gabriel announced the birth of Jesus. De Faverches was told to build a copy of the house in Walsingham, which she did. The structure de Faverches built became the site of a pilgrimage for Christians from near and far. Many people still visit the site each year.

The Western Wall

One of the world's most visited pilgrim sites is a 2000-year-old section of wall. Known as the Western Wall, it lies in the Old City of Jerusalem in Israel. While it is important to many religions, including Christianity, it is an especially important place for Jewish people. The wall was built to surround the Second Temple by King Herod in 520 BCE. It was destroyed by Roman forces in 70 CE.

The Western Wall is almost all that is left of the Second Temple. It is the most important **holy** site in **Judaism**. Jews believe that the rebuilding of the Temple will be one of the signs that the **Messiah** has come.

This is a model of the Second Temple of Jerusalem before its destruction.

This pilgrim visiting the Western Wall is a rabbi (Jewish religious leader) who has journeyed all the way from South Africa.

Each year many Jews visit the Western Wall to say prayers. Some even push their written-down prayers into holes in the wall. They believe that this will mean their prayers have a better chance of being answered by god.

Daniel's story

Thirteen-year-old Daniel Gamon visited the Western Wall with his father in July 2002:

'*It was amazing to see, knowing that it had been there for two thousand years. What was even more exciting was that while we were there the Wall began to leak. People told us that when the Western Wall leaks it's a sign that the Messiah is coming.*

'*We saw lots of other places in Jerusalem, but the Wall was the best. Even hearing that the damp patch might have been caused by a leaking pipe didn't spoil it!*'

Pesach

Pesach (say 'Pey-sak') is an annual seven or eight-day holiday celebrated by **Jewish** people. (It lasts for seven days inside Israel, and usually for eight days elsewhere.) The holiday – which is known as a pilgrim festival – remembers the time about 3000 years ago when the Jews made a great journey. At this time the Jews were slaves of the Egyptian pharaoh (king). The Jewish leader Moses asked the pharaoh to free the Jews. Finally, after God had sent ten terrible **plagues** to the Egyptians, the pharaoh agreed. The Jews left so suddenly that they did not even have time to bake bread for their journey. Instead they heated unbaked dough in the sun as they travelled. In memory of this, Jews eat unleavened bread (flat bread, made without yeast) during Pesach.

This painting shows the Jews escaping from slavery by crossing the Red Sea. God had parted the waters for them, and then closed them again to drown the following Egyptians.

Today, Jewish people often try to be with their families for Pesach. Children journey home to their parents' house. Brothers and sisters, cousins and nephews travel to be together. Other Jews make a journey to the Western Wall in Jerusalem.

A Jewish family in Jerusalem celebrate the Seder meal together. The man standing up is retelling the story of the Jewish escape from slavery.

The Seder meal

Seder is a special meal eaten on the first two nights of Pesach. First, the story of the Jews' escape from Egypt is retold. Then the meal begins. Special foods are eaten in a particular order. These special foods include:

- *matzah* – or unleavened bread
- *maror* – 'bitter herbs', which stand for the bitterness of slavery
- *baitzah* – a hard-boiled egg, which stands for the cycle of life
- *zaroah* – a roasted lamb bone
- *haroset* – a mixture of chopped nuts, apples and wine, which remembers the clay used by the Jewish slaves to make bricks
- *karpas* – parsley, lettuce or other green plants, which stand for the freshness of new life.

Four cups of wine are also drunk at key moments. A full cup of wine is also left on the table – waiting for the **prophet** Elijah. If he appears to drink his wine, it is a sign that the **Messiah** is coming.

Pilgrimage to Varanasi

On the banks of the River Ganges in northern India sits the city of Varanasi (also called Benares). This is one of the seven **holy** cities of the **Hindu** religion. Ancient writings mention that even 3000 years ago Varanasi was a place of learning. The city also appears in the Mahabharata (say 'Maa-habba-ratta') and the Ramayana (say 'Ramma-yanna'), the two most important pieces of writing in the Hindu religion.

Temples and gods

There are over 1500 temples in Varanasi, which is one for every 650 people who live there. The temples are popular with pilgrims, who go there to worship. Each temple is home to at least one form of god, who appears there as a deity. Each day the god is woken with bells, purified with incense, bathed, dressed and fed, before going to sleep again that night.

Cleansing away sin

The River Ganges is holy to Hindus. Each year many thousands of them journey to Varanasi to bathe in the river and say prayers. They do this because they believe that bathing in the holy river will wash away their sins. The Varanasi ghats are very popular. Ghats are stone steps used by pilgrims to go down to the water to bathe.

Four out of every five people in India are Hindus. People journey from all over the country to bathe in the Ganges at Varanasi. Some make the **pilgrimage** as hard as possible, by crawling part of the way. Many Hindus who live in other countries also come on a pilgrimage. Each morning worshippers walk down the ghats to bathe.

These Hindus are bathing in the River Ganges.
They hope that the river will clean away their sins.

Sikh journeys

In the city of Amritsar, in the Punjab region of north-western India, there is a lake called Amrit Sarowar. Its name means 'the Pool of Immortality'. In the middle of the lake is the holiest place in the **Sikh** religion – the Harmandir Sahib (Golden Temple). The temple is covered in gold leaf (foil).

Many Sikhs and people of other backgrounds visit the Golden Temple each year. There are some hand-written Siri Guru Granth Sahibs (say 'si-ree goo-roo gran-th sar-hib') in the temple. The Siri Guru Granth Sahib is the **holy** scripture of the Sikh faith. It is stored inside the temple. While most Sikhs live in the Punjab, there are many more living in other countries too, and some of them also come to the Golden Temple.

The Golden Temple in Amritsar, the most holy place in the world for Sikhs. Many thousands journey here each year.

Guru Nanak's travels

Today's pilgrims journey by aeroplane or car, bus or train.
Guru Nanak (1469–1539) had four great journeys, which
took him all across the Punjab and northern India. He tried
to combine parts of different religions into one religion that
all people could follow equally.

These pilgrims are arriving at the gates of the Golden Temple, where their holy book, the Siri Guru Granth Sahib, is kept.

Nanak and the Brahmins

One day Guru Nanak found himself on the banks of the River
Ganges. Standing in the river was a group of Brahmins (Hindu
priests). They were throwing water at the sun to quench the souls of
their **ancestors**. Nanak waded in and began to throw water in the
opposite direction. He told the Brahmins he was watering his fields in
the Punjab. They began to mock Nanak, until he replied that if their
water could reach the Sun, his could certainly cover a few hundred
kilometres to the Punjab.

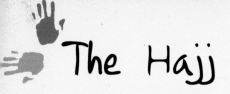

The Hajj

Each year millions of pilgrims journey to the city of Makkah in Saudi Arabia. They are **Muslims**, followers of the Islamic religion. Islam is based on five 'pillars', the five duties of all Muslims. One of the five duties is to visit Makkah if this is possible. This **pilgrimage** to Makkah is called the Hajj (say 'Hadd-j').

Makkah is the city where Muhammad (pbuh), the final **prophet** of Islam, was born. It is Islam's most **holy** city. Each year over two million Muslims arrive during the month of pilgrimage. They come from all over the world.

The area around the Great Mosque, at the heart of Islam's holiest city, Makkah.

Worshipping together with so many other Muslims during the Hajj is an experience people bring to their own mosques when they return home.

At the heart of the city is the Great **Mosque**, which can hold over a million people. In the courtyard of the mosque is the Kaaba (say 'Ka-ah-bah'). This word means 'a square building' in Arabic. The Kaaba is the most important pilgrim site in Makkah. The Qur'an (say 'kor-ARN'), the Muslim holy book, says that it was built to God's plan. Inside is the Black Stone, one of the most holy objects for Muslims. The Black Stone is said to have been given to humans on behalf of God by the angel Gabriel. All Muslims face in the direction of Makkah and the Kaaba five times a day, during their prayers.

Jamal's story

Jamal Hussein, thirteen years old, remembers his journey to Makkah:

'My father took me to Makkah for the Hajj last year. It was amazing – so many people crammed together in such a small space! As we moved from one place to another in a huge crowd, everyone was part of the same thing, all part of our religion together. I hope that one day I can go back and perform the Hajj again.'

A journey of prostration

In the south-western corner of the Chinese province of Tibet stands Mount Kailash. The mountain is **holy** to **Buddhists**, who think it is the centre of the universe. Each year many Buddhists visit Mount Kailash, hoping to walk round it. By making this difficult journey around the holy mountain they believe they gain merit, or **spiritual** reward.

This traveller is clapping his hands together in the first part of a prostration. Repeated again and again as part of a pilgrimage, this tiring way of moving forward is thought to be especially good.

A hard path

The path around the mountain is 52 kilometres long, and it is about 4500 metres above sea level. At this height there is less oxygen in the air. Each breath provides the body with less oxygen, so walkers get out of breath and tired far faster than down at sea level. The weather on the mountain is also very hard to predict. It is often bitterly cold, windy and snowy.

To gain extra merit, many Buddhists travel the path by making prostrations as they go. This involves clapping their hands together above their head, then moving them down their body before falling forward on to their hands and knees. Once they have slid out to full-length on the ground, they can stand up and start to make the next prostration. Completing the whole path around Mount Kailash in this way can take several weeks.

These pilgrims are making a journey through the tough country around Mount Kailash.

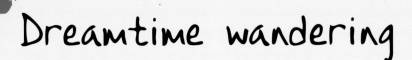

Dreamtime wandering

Traditional Australian Aborigines believe the world was created during the Dreamtime when the **Ancestors**, including a wallaby and a crocodile, made themselves out of clay. Every Aborigine believes that they are a member of a **clan** started in the Dreamtime by one of the Ancestors.

Some Aborigines can still follow their clan's Songline today.

Ancestral footsteps

As the Ancestors travelled around Australia, they sang out the names of the things and creatures that crossed their paths. By doing this, the Ancestors sang the world into existence. At the same time, they scattered behind them trails of words and musical notes that made up a song. These songs were taught to members of their clan, and used as a map to follow the path the Ancestor had taken. Since every feature of the landscape was mentioned in the song, it provided a guide to where the Ancestor had walked.

According to Aboriginal beliefs, these song-paths criss-cross the whole landscape of Australia. Aborigines call them 'Footsteps of the Ancestors' or 'Way of the Law'. Most Europeans know them as 'Songlines'. Although today many of the songs have been lost, some still survive. It is still possible for an Aborigine who knows the song of his clan to sing his way across the countryside, following the footsteps of his Ancestor.

Songlines conflict

Because the ancient routes of the Songlines are **sacred** to Aboriginal people, they can cause problems with non-Aborigines. Building a new road, for example, could cut a Songline apart, rubbing out the footsteps of the Ancestors and making the path impossible to follow.

Boulders, like this one at the Devil's Marbles in Australia's Northern Territory, can be important markers on a Songline.

Mountain journeys

Some mountains are climbed for religious reasons – Croagh Patrick in Ireland, for example. Saint Patrick is the patron saint of Ireland. In **Christianity**, a patron saint is thought to protect a particular place or activity. According to legend Saint Patrick stayed on the summit (highest point) of Croagh Patrick for 40 days without eating. Today, people come from all over the world to climb Croagh Patrick on 'Reek Sunday' (the last Sunday in July). They do this to celebrate Saint Patrick's great feat.

The statue of St Patrick on Croagh Patrick in Ireland. Thousands of people climb the mountain on St Patrick's Day, some of them barefoot.

Base Camp at Everest, the world's highest mountain. Each year hundreds of climbers travel to the mountain, hoping to reach its summit.

Other mountains are climbed for personal reasons. The journey up the mountain and back is still a bit like a **pilgrimage** for the people who make it. Each year thousands of people visit the base of Mount Everest, in the Himalayas. Everest is **sacred** to the Sherpa people, who live in the region. The Sherpa act as guides for the tourists who visit Everest. Their name for it is Chomolungma, which means 'goddess mother'.

To most people, Everest is no more than the world's tallest mountain. Nonetheless, many people have lost their lives trying to climb it. Among them is George Mallory, who never made it back from his attempt to reach the summit. Other mountaineers have also paid with their lives for their journeys in the Alps, the Rockies, Andes and other mountain ranges around the world.

The value of journeys

Why do people make the special journeys that are talked about in this book? 'There are two kinds of men in the world – those that stay at home and those that do not,' said the English writer Rudyard Kipling. He meant that some people have a need to travel, and become miserable if they cannot.

Climbers on Mont Blanc, France, Europe's highest mountain. Millions of people climb mountains for fun every year.

Animal instinct

In nature, the need to travel is even stronger than among some humans. The scientist Charles Darwin gave the example of Audubon's goose. If its pinion feathers are removed the goose cannot fly on its annual migration (movement to another place to feed or breed). Instead, the goose starts to walk, even though it could never finish the journey.

The Kumbh Mela festival in India, January 2001. Holy men and women, as well as other Hindus, come together to bathe in the River Ganges. The festival takes place every twelve years.

An ancient Moorish **proverb** says that: 'He who does not travel does not know the value of men.' It means that only by travelling is it possible to find out what people are really like: whether they are kind, cruel, mean or generous. But travellers also find out about themselves. When faced with a long walk they discover how determined they can be, even when tired. When a fellow traveller has no food or water, they discover how generous they can be, even if they are hungry themselves. And most of all, travellers carrying all their equipment on their back find out how little they really need.

This might be why travelling is important in most religions. By travelling, religious people realize that they need little more than a few possessions and the company of their god.

Glossary

ancestor relative in the past. Your grandparents and great-grandparents are your ancestors.

apostle one of the twelve followers of Jesus

Buddhists (Buddhism) people who follow the way of life taught by the Buddha, who lived in ancient India about 2500 years ago. The Buddha was not a god, but a man. He taught his followers how to live simple, peaceful lives.

Christians (Christianity) people who follow the religion of Christianity, which is based on the teachings of Jesus Christ. Christians believe that Jesus was the Son of God.

clan group of people who are all related to one another by birth or marriage

crucified way of killing criminals used by the Romans and others. The criminal was tied to a wooden cross, nails were driven through his hands and feet, and he was left to die.

Hindus (Hinduism) people who follow Hinduism. Hindus worship one god (called Brahman) in many forms. Hinduism is the main religion in India.

holy special because it is to do with God or a religious purpose

Jews (Judaism) people who follow the religion of Judaism. Jews pray to one god. Their holy book is the Hebrew Bible, sometimes called the Old Testament by Christians.

Mass religious ceremony held by members of the Roman Catholic part of the Christian religion

Messiah person who saves a people who are enslaved; particularly important idea within Judaism

mosque Muslim place of worship

Muslims (Islam) people who follow the religion of Islam. Muslims pray to one god, whom they call Allah.

pilgrimage journey to a special, often religious, site. A person who goes on a pilgrimage is called a pilgrim.

plague great trouble, usually some sort of infectious disease, from which many people suffer

prophet religious teacher, instructed by God

proverb a short saying that usually includes a well-known truth

sacred having spiritual or religious importance

Sikhs (Sikhism) people who follow the religion of Sikhism, based on the teachings of the ten Gurus, or teachers

sin action or thought that is against religious laws. A sinner is someone who commits a sin or sins.

spiritual of the world of the spirit (soul) rather than the physical world

Virgin Mary in Christianity, the human mother of Jesus

Further resources

More books to read
Hindu Stories, Anita Ganeri (Evans Brothers, 2000)

Pilgrimages and Journeys, Sue Kendall
(Hodder Wayland, 2001)

Religions of the World (series), Sue Penney
(Heinemann Library 2002)

Websites
www.dreamtime.net.au
Retellings of stories from the Dreamtime by Aborigine people

www.sacredsites.com
Contains information on various **sacred** places, including a good article on the **pilgrimage** sites of India.

Index

Titles in the *Rites of Passage* series include:

Hardback   0 431 17715 5

Hardback   0 431 17711 2

Hardback   0 431 17712 0

Hardback   0 431 17713 9

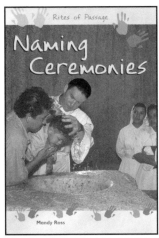

Hardback   0 431 17710 4

Hardback   0 431 17714 7

Find out about the other titles in this series on our website www.heinemann.co.uk/library